IT'S TIME TO LEARN ABOUT CHIMPANZEES

It's Time to Learn about Chimpanzees

Walter the Educator

Silent King Books
A WhichHead Entertainment Imprint

Copyright © 2025 by Walter the Educator

All rights reserved. No part of this book may be reproduced in any manner whatsoever without written per- mission except in the case of brief quotations embodied in critical articles and reviews.

First Printing, 2024

Disclaimer

This book is a literary work; the story is not about specific persons, locations, situations, and/or circumstances unless mentioned in a historical context. Any resemblance to real persons, locations, situations, and/or circumstances is coincidental. This book is for entertainment and informational purposes only. The author and publisher offer this information without warranties expressed or implied. No matter the grounds, neither the author nor the publisher will be accountable for any losses, injuries, or other damages caused by the reader's use of this book. The use of this book acknowledges an understanding and acceptance of this disclaimer.

It's Time to Learn about Chimpanzees is a collectible early learning book by Walter the Educator suitable for all ages belonging to Walter the Educator's Time to Eat Book Series. Collect more books at WaltertheEducator.com

USE THE EXTRA SPACE TO TAKE NOTES AND DOCUMENT YOUR MEMORIES

CHIMPANZEES

Chimpanzees are clever apes,

It's Time to Learn about
Chimpanzees

They swing through trees in daring shapes.

They live in groups called "troops," you see,

Deep in the jungles, wild and free!

Their arms are long, their fingers strong,

They climb and play the whole day long.

They swing on vines and leap with glee

The kings and queens of canopy!

They do not bark, they do not meow,

They hoot and grunt and sometimes growl.

With calls and sounds and claps and squeals,

They tell each other how they feel.

Chimpanzees are smart and wise,

They make tools right before your eyes!

A stick for bugs, a stone for nuts

They never miss when lunchtime cuts.

It's Time to Learn about
Chimpanzees

They munch on fruit and leaves so green,

And sometimes bugs that can't be seen.

They love to eat, they love to share,

Their food is found most everywhere!

They play with friends, they hug and groom,

They chase and laugh and make some room.

They care for young with love so true,

Like moms and dads and families do.

Though chimps are fun, you must beware

They're wild and strong and best with care.

You shouldn't keep one as a pet,

They belong in forests, safe and set.

Some chimps are shy and some are bold,

They live in places hot and old.

In Africa they make their home,

It's Time to Learn about Chimpanzees

Where baobab and fig trees roam.

They're cousins close to you and me,

We share a lot, just wait and see!

Our DNA is much the same,

We're part of nature's wondrous game.

So if you hear a chimpanzee,

Say "hello" from you and me.

Protect their forests, keep them safe,

It's Time to Learn about
Chimpanzees

For every chimp's a treasure place!

ABOUT THE CREATOR

Walter the Educator is one of the pseudonyms for Walter Anderson. Formally educated in Chemistry, Business, and Education, he is an educator, an author, a diverse entrepreneur, and he is the son of a disabled war veteran. "Walter the Educator" shares his time between educating and creating. He holds interests and owns several creative projects that entertain, enlighten, enhance, and educate, hoping to inspire and motivate you. Follow, find new works, and stay up to date with Walter the Educator™ at WaltertheEducator.com

www.ingramcontent.com/pod-product-compliance
Lightning Source LLC
LaVergne TN
LVHW051920060526
838201LV00060B/4090